My 12-Step Journey
Recovery Workbook

Denise DeNicolo

Copyright © 2019 by Denise DeNicolo

All rights reserved. By purchase of this book, you have been licensed one copy for personal use only. No part of this publication may be reproduced, distributed or transmitted in any form or by any means, including photocopying, recording, or other electronic or mechanical methods, without the prior written permission of the copyright owner.

Brock Haus Press

My 12-Step Journey: Recovery Workbook | Denise DeNicolo
ISBN: 978-1-7340926-0-8

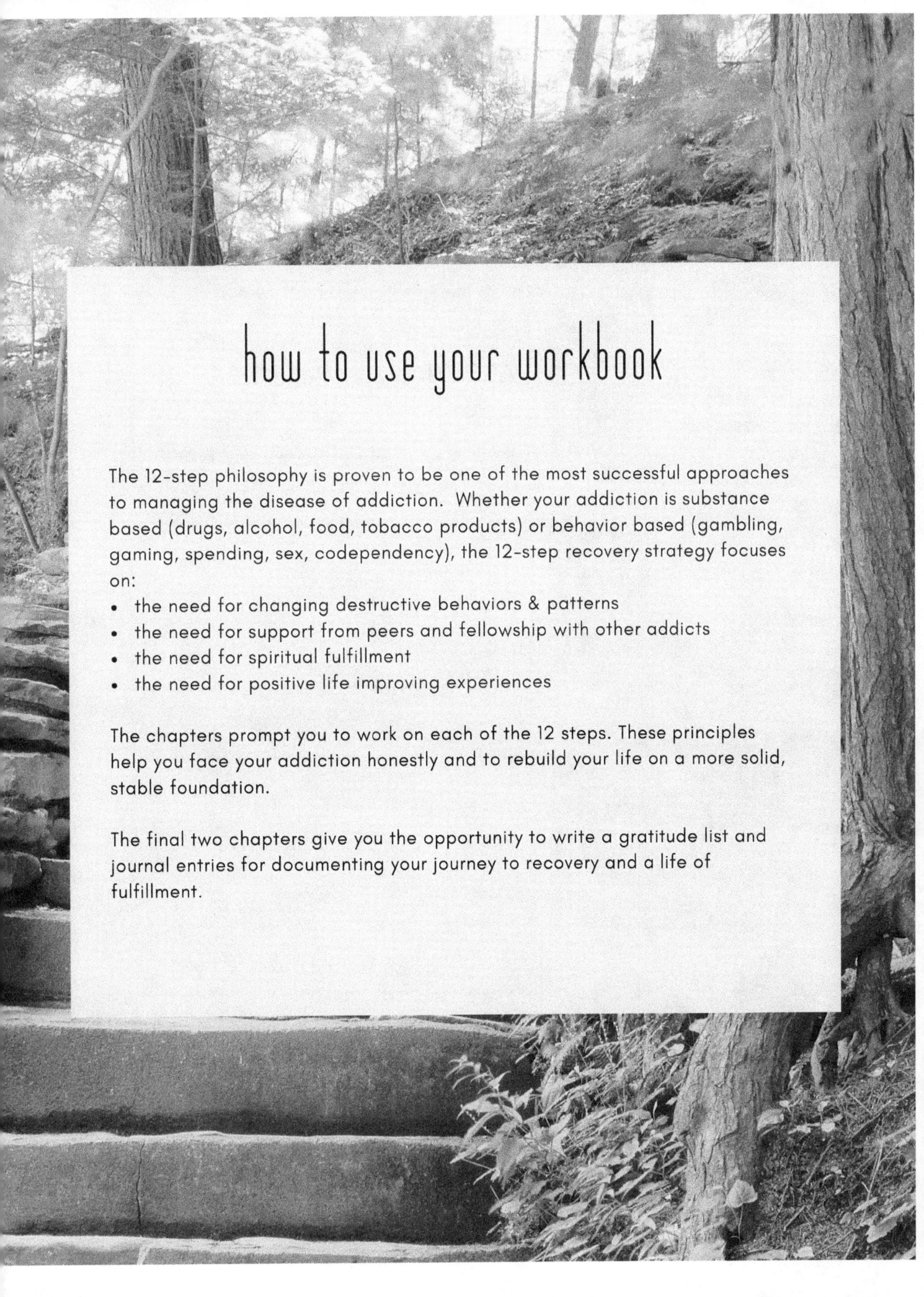

how to use your workbook

The 12-step philosophy is proven to be one of the most successful approaches to managing the disease of addiction. Whether your addiction is substance based (drugs, alcohol, food, tobacco products) or behavior based (gambling, gaming, spending, sex, codependency), the 12-step recovery strategy focuses on:

- the need for changing destructive behaviors & patterns
- the need for support from peers and fellowship with other addicts
- the need for spiritual fulfillment
- the need for positive life improving experiences

The chapters prompt you to work on each of the 12 steps. These principles help you face your addiction honestly and to rebuild your life on a more solid, stable foundation.

The final two chapters give you the opportunity to write a gratitude list and journal entries for documenting your journey to recovery and a life of fulfillment.

TABLE OF CONTENTS

STEP 1 — ACCEPTANCE – Page 1

STEP 2 — HOPE – Page 7

STEP 3 — WILLINGNESS – Page 13

STEP 4 — PERSONAL INVENTORY – Page 19

TABLE OF CONTENTS

STEP 5 — SELF DISCLOSURE – Page 25

STEP 6 — REFLECTING – Page 31

STEP 7 — HUMILITY – Page 37

STEP 8 — AMENDS LIST – Page 43

TABLE OF CONTENTS

STEP 9 — MADE AMENDS – Page 49

STEP 10 — CONTINUED INVENTORY – Page 55

STEP 11 — SPIRITUAL GROWTH – Page 61

STEP 12 — GIVING BACK – Page 67

We admitted we were powerless over our addiction, that our lives had become unmanageable.

Fully recognize your powerlessness over your addiction and your inability to control your life and your behavior through self-will alone. The process of surrender is the first step in your recovery.

Date started this step:_____

_____
_____
_____
_____
_____
_____
_____
_____
_____
_____
_____
_____
_____
_____
_____
_____
_____

Came to believe that a power greater than ourselves could restore us to sanity.

This step is designed to prepare you for the solution to come in steps three through twelve. It introduces you to the general nature of the long-term solution: that you will need to accept outside help.

Date started this step:_____

_____
_____
_____
_____
_____
_____
_____
_____
_____
_____
_____
_____
_____
_____
_____

Made a decision to turn our will and our lives over to the care of God as we understood Him.

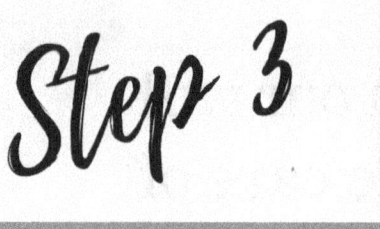

Understand that a higher power, whether you call it "God", "higher power", or something else, can be anything outside of yourself that helps you stay sober. For many recovering addicts, "GOD" is an acronym for the "Good Orderly Direction" provided by advisors and support network.

Date started this step: _____

_____
_____
_____
_____
_____
_____
_____
_____
_____
_____
_____
_____
_____
_____
_____
_____
_____
_____
_____

Made a searching and fearless moral inventory of ourselves.

Be honest about your moral defects. They give you insight as to why you started using in the first place. Drop the word "blame" from your vocabulary. You and you alone are responsible for your behaviors. This is where you list your "stinking thinking".

Date started this step:_____

Admitted to God, to ourselves, and to another human being the exact nature of our wrongs.

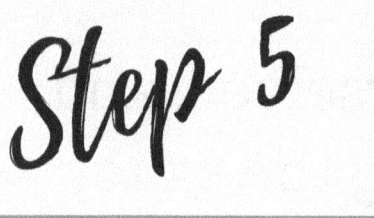

You will feel a huge weight lifted once you confide in another. Reveal your most distressing and tormenting memories to another person. Be honest. Accept the advice from that person with an open mind. Let go of reservations and don't worry about being judged for what you have done. Choose someone you're comfortable with.

Date started this step: _____

Were entirely ready to have God remove all these defects of character.

Become fully prepared to rid yourself of the flaws you listed in Step 4. This step reveals character and your true willingness to recover. You're a work in progress. Be happy about your success so far and celebrate each little victory. Keep an open mind and a positive attitude throughout your journey.

Date started this step: _____

Humbly asked Him to remove all our shortcomings.

You cannot overcome your character flaws without humility. Begin to practice modesty and welcome a change of attitude which will lead to a happy life. It's important to feel the pain you masked with drugs and alcohol. Be patient. You can't change your life overnight.

Date started this step:_____

Made a list of all persons we had harmed, and became willing to make amends to them all.

Make a list of everyone you have hurt and how you hurt them. Pay attention to what you discover about yourself and your problems along the way. Don't be defensive or blame others for how they treated you. Forgive them, because without forgiving others, you cannot forgive yourself.

Date started this step:_____

Made direct amends to such people wherever possible, except when to do so would injure them or others.

Take action and apologize to those you have harmed due to your substance use. This step will provide you with peace of mind, relief and liberation from the chains of regret.

Date started this step: _____

Continued to take personal inventory and when we were wrong promptly admitted it.

Examine yourself as part of your daily routine. Just as you've addressed your defects, keep your successes in check. Correction of your wrongs is not a one-time thing. Make self-evaluation a timeless habit. Assess your situation honestly. Admit when you're wrong. Forgive others when they're wrong. Focus on progress not perfection.

Date started this step: _____

_____
_____
_____
_____
_____
_____
_____
_____
_____
_____
_____
_____
_____
_____
_____
_____
_____

Sought through prayer and meditation to improve our conscious contact with God as we understood Him, praying only for knowledge of His will for us and the power to carry that out.

 Create a solid foundation for a peaceful and fulfilled life. Develop a more positive way of thinking. A daily spiritual practice promotes emotional balance and stability.

Date started this step:_____

___
___
___
___
___
___
___
___
___
___
___
___
___
___
___
___
___

Having had a spiritual awakening as the result of these steps, we tried to carry this message to alcoholics and to practice these principles in all our affairs.

Help others. Reach out to those who are suffering. Give selflessly and ask for nothing in return. Practice all twelve steps on a daily basis as a foundation for your new life. Learn to find peace within yourself with whatever life throws your way.

Date started this step:_____

GRATITUDE LIST

POSITIVE

Everyone has something to be grateful for; writing it down can boost your happiness.

JOURNAL ENTRIES

POSITIVE

There are benefits of journaling for your health, happiness and productivity.

Serenity Prayer

God,

Grant me the

Serenity

to accept the things I cannot change, the

Courage

to change the things I can, the

Wisdom

to know the difference.